IMAGES
of America

FORT DES MOINES

This aerial view of Fort Des Moines in 1942 reveals the original fort, dating back to 1901, in the upper left quadrant surrounding the parade ground. In the lower right quadrant is the area built in 1942 for the Women's Army Auxiliary Corps (WAAC). Originally called the Winn Area, the WAAC renamed it Boomtown because its row upon row of temporary buildings seemed to boom into existence overnight. (Courtesy U.S. Army Women's Museum, Fort Lee, Virginia.)

On the cover: Proudly wearing their new fatigue uniforms, these scores of members of the WAAC form ranks in front of the barracks at their new training school at Fort Des Moines. These women are a part of the first 800 members of the WAAC to arrive at the fort in July 1942. (AP/Wide World Photos.)

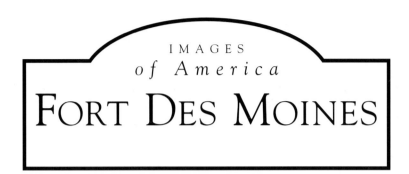

IMAGES
of America

FORT DES MOINES

Penelope A. LeFew-Blake, Ph.D.

ARCADIA
PUBLISHING

This book is dedicated to my mother, Capt. Carrie A. LeFew (née Jones), WAAC/WAC, 1942–1946, who served at Fort Des Moines throughout World War II. Many photographs from her private collection appear in this book.

CONTENTS

ACKNOWLEDGMENTS

I wish to thank first and foremost my research assistant and best friend, Candice Haffner Joern, who traveled with me to Fort Des Moines each year to aid me in my research. I also wish to acknowledge the following individuals for their photographs and invaluable firsthand information about Fort Des Moines: Rosemary Reed Powell, former Fort Des Moines Women's Army Corps member and my mother's best friend; Dr. Eugene and Jewel Marsh, former residents of the fort during World War II; and cartoonist Max Halverson for his wonderful illustrations and stories about the fort.

I wish to acknowledge Col. Louis Erbstein, curator of the Fort Des Moines Memorial Park and Education Center, for his informative guidance and several detailed tours of the current fort, as well as for his exhaustive efforts to preserve the fort's history. My gratitude extends also to Jack Lufkin of the Iowa Historical Society for answering so many questions and to the curators of the Women's Military Museum at Fort Lee, Virginia, Britta K. Granrud at the Women in Service for America Memorial in Arlington, Virginia, and the *Des Moines Register* archivists for their assistance in locating original photographs of the fort.

Finally, I send many thanks to John Pearson, my editor at Arcadia Publishing, for his endless patience and professional expertise in answering my questions and guiding me through this process.

INTRODUCTION

Fort Des Moines first evolved as a means of protecting white settlements from Native American attacks along the Raccoon and Des Moines Rivers, and in 1843, the fort stood at the fork of these two rivers. An Indian agent at Fort Leavenworth, Kansas, John Dougherty, recommended that a military garrison be established at the location, and in May 1843, Capt. James Allen and a company of 200 U.S. dragoons built and occupied the fort. Originally named Fort Raccoon, the fortification was renamed Fort Des Moines at the directive of Gen. Winfield Scott. The name "Des Moines" has no direct translation but is probably a combination of the Native American and French names for the river, Moingonia ("river of the mounds") and La Rivere des Moines ("river in the middle"). The early fort attracted civilian settlers in the area (currently the site of the Sec Taylor Stadium), and a community gradually evolved. When the threat of attack diminished with the relocation of Native American tribes by the U.S. government in 1846, the river fort was abandoned but evolved into what became the actual city of Des Moines by 1857. Later that same year, the city became the capital of Iowa.

The 20th century soon offered its own challenges to the area, and by 1901, a fort proved necessary once again, this time built in its present location, approximately four miles south of Des Moines. Using Congressional authorization to raise funds, the people of Des Moines claimed responsibility for the construction and upkeep of the fort. Even though the site lacked a sufficient water supply, local citizens took on the daily task of providing water to the fort, and the red brick that created the fort's unique structures also came from local suppliers. Because of their large investment in the fort, the people of Des Moines came to regard it as their own, a gathering place for civic meetings, family picnics, and patriotic fireworks on the Fourth of July.

By 1903, the fort had become a cavalry post, the largest in the country at that time. Its distinctive red brick barracks, officers' quarters, horse stables, and post exchange nestled in over 400 acres of expansive green fields and meadows created a pastoral, agrarian landscape seldom seen at military installations. From its inception, then, Fort Des Moines was renowned for its beauty and sense of Old World grace, which would at times belie the purpose of its existence: to train men, and later women, to defend themselves and their country in time of war. With each year and each new building, the fort grew lovelier and more acclaimed throughout the country as the jewel, the "West Point," of the Midwest.

Almost immediately after its official dedication on November 13, 1903, which included an extravagant barbecue for over 22,000 people, Fort Des Moines began to take a central place in the annals of American military history when the first African American troops arrived. During the winter months of 1903, two companies of the all-black 25th Infantry quartered at the post. Since the city of Des Moines had evolved as a racially diverse city almost from its inception, Fort Des Moines would play a revolutionary role in the movement toward diversity and, eventually, integration in the U.S. military.

Until the beginning of U.S. involvement in World War I, Fort Des Moines grew as a premier cavalry post. Units from all over the country arrived at the fort to train. In 1909, Pres. William Howard Taft visited the fort to present awards to the winners of the Great Cavalry Tournament, a competition among several units from various posts. Since much of the nation's military strength rested on cavalry troops, the importance of such a fine venue as Fort Des Moines for cavalry maneuvers, training, and housing cannot be overstated. Still, because the years preceding World War I were relatively peaceful ones for the United States, the cavalry was seldom called to action. In 1911, the entire Fort Des Moines regiment was ordered to border control duty as a revolution raged in Mexico, and the fort stood silent for a time. When the United States entered World War I in 1917, Fort Des Moines gradually decreased its cavalry holdings and focused on housing and training black officers. In 1917, for the first time in American history, 639 African American officers received commissions at Fort Des Moines.

After World War I, the fort experienced yet another transformation. In 1918, Fort Des Moines became a hospital, treating wounded soldiers as they returned from Europe. Training facilities for hospital personnel, many of whom were African American, were also set up at the fort. The barracks and stables were partially converted into hospital wards.

"The War to End All Wars" had clearly signaled the end of an era in the methods of conducting warfare, away from the horse-driven conflicts of cavalry troops toward modern battle techniques and machinery. As the military marched into the new world of radios, telephones, electricity, and the automobile, the cavalry soldier became an anachronism. Even so, Fort Des Moines reopened as a cavalry post and field artillery training facility in 1920. The stables once again rustled with the sounds of horse hoofs, and the parade ground, drill fields, and polo grounds filled with soldiers on horseback simulating Rough Rider charges (future president Ronald Reagan learned to ride with the cavalry at Fort Des Moines, receiving his commission as second lieutenant in 1937). Meanwhile, the military establishment signed off on plans to bring this world to an end and replace it with the roar and wonder of tanks, airplanes, and immense warships. By 1940, the government converted Fort Des Moines into a training field for artillery regiments, transforming the stables into garages for motorized vehicles and equipment. The cavalry rode most of its 500 horses out of Fort Des Moines that year, never to return.

By 1941, with the storm clouds of war once again on the horizon, Rep. Edith Nourse Rogers of Massachusetts, with the support of First Lady Eleanor Roosevelt, introduced a bill that would provide for an "auxiliary corps of women" to fill the thousands of noncombat roles in the military—accountants, cooks, motor pool drivers, switchboard operators, interpreters, librarians, headquarters administrators, post exchange officers—all of which had been filled previously by men now desperately needed for combat roles. On May 14, 1942, Congress passed Rogers's bill, giving birth to the Women's Army Auxiliary Corps (WAAC), reclassified on September 30, 1943, as the Women's Army Corps (WAC). (Throughout this book, members of the Women's Army Auxiliary Corps are referred to as WAACs, and members of the Women's Army Corps are referred to as WACs.)

Soon recruiting centers were overrun with enthusiastic women eager to join the war effort. Planners had to reassess their original estimates: they had forecast a gradual increase of the number of WAACs from 12,000 the first year to 25,000 the second, and 62,000 by the end of 1944. Instead, the number of WAACs by the end of the first year reached over 60,000. With such overwhelming numbers of potential recruits, the military had to address an immediate concern: where would they train?

The old cavalry post and current induction center at Fort Des Moines seemed the best option, despite its extreme weather: hot, steamy summers and wickedly cold winters. The fort's location just outside of a major city with an airport and several train lines simplified transportation and supply issues, and the city's buildings could be used to house and school the overflow of WAACs until the fort could be expanded sufficiently. Fort Des Moines was also located near the geographic center of the country, had no major defense projects in operation at the time (other than the induction center, which could be relocated to nearby Fort Dodge), would present no race issues (10 percent of the WAAC would be African American), and, most importantly, offered the space and structures necessary to accommodate the WAAC, with only minimal renovations (in the barracks formerly used by cavalry officers, once the urinals were replaced with toilets, the barracks were functional for the WAAC). Of course, the nine huge cavalry stables, quickly converted to barracks, would play a major role in this capability. In fact, the legacy of the cavalry lingered in more than one way. When the first WAACs arrived at Fort Des Moines in 1942 and found themselves quartered in the former cavalry stables, many commented on the unmistakable scent of horseflesh wafting through the air of their new home.

Although one of the advantages of Fort Des Moines was its many extant military buildings, including barracks, a post exchange, a guardhouse, administration buildings, a headquarters building, officers' quarters, and a hospital, changes and additions were necessary to accommodate the first group of nearly 800 WAACs scheduled to arrive by late summer. In addition to the changes in bathroom facilities, the fort was enlarged with new quarters for nurses in the hospital area, an additional officers' mess hall, and two officers' quarters, as well as a chapel, theater, two service clubs, and a post library.

Overall construction increased by 20 percent, including an area officially called Winn Area after Gen. John S. Winn, a famous artillery officer. WAACs later named the area Boomtown to describe the way it boomed into existence. Located at the south end of the original fort, Boomtown provided housing, support facilities, and classrooms for the new WAAC: 112 buildings sprung up in less than five months, averaging 16 buildings a week. The total structures built in Boomtown reached 174, more buildings than many of the women saw in their hometowns. But although the area seemed to appear overnight, its growth was actually messy and difficult, especially as the WAACs arrived before Boomtown was completed. The unpaved, muddy roads in Boomtown would figure prominently and comically in many WAACs' letters and photographs home.

Following World War II, much of Fort Des Moines was demolished, acres of land sold to private, corporate, or governmental concerns. A few buildings that remain today serve as a naval reserve center, and Clayton Hall is the centerpiece of the Fort Des Moines Memorial Park and Education Center. The center opened in 2004, and its museum features artifacts and documents pertaining to the central role Fort Des Moines played in changing the U.S. military in terms of its acceptance of minorities and women. The legacy of Fort Des Moines lives on in the thousands of women and minorities who today serve with equal rank and privileges in all branches of the U.S. military.

One

CALVARY AND THE
HOSPITAL YEARS
1843–1942

The original site of Fort Des Moines, established in 1843, was located at the fork of the Raccoon and Des Moines Rivers. Built as a means of protecting white settlements from Native American attacks, the fort became the nucleus around which the city of Des Moines developed. The fort itself was evacuated in 1846.

North Gate, Ft. Des Moines, Des Moines, Iowa.

By 1901, a second fort was built on the site it occupies today, located approximately four miles south of Des Moines. The North Gate, seen here, served as one of the two main entrances to the fort. While the gate itself changed in design and structure through the years, some kind of sentinel station or small guardhouse always stood nearby the entrance, as seen on the right of this photograph.

Beyond the North Gate, the officers' quarters stand, lining the north side of the parade ground. Built in the distinctive red brick of all of the fort's original buildings, these beautiful, noble structures contributed to the fort's reputation as the "West Point" of the Midwest.

By 1909, a line of officers' barracks had been built along the north side of the parade ground. This area came to be known as "Officers' Row."

The young trees in front of Officers' Row, seen here in 1909, later provided the lush green canopies around Fort Des Moines and created what many likened to a country club atmosphere.

The Officers Candidate School (OCS) barracks lined the south side of the parade ground, opposite Officers' Row, in 1909.

These OCS barracks, pictured in 1910, featured three floors, two-level porch areas, and large first-floor rooms capable of serving both as barracks as well as halls of entertainment, including dancing and piano playing.

The main post exchange (PX No. 1), featured here in the foreground in 1910, was one of the first buildings erected at Fort Des Moines. Soldiers returning from World War I and World War II would seek refreshments and basic supplies within its walls. The headquarters building, also one of the earliest buildings constructed at the fort, can be seen in the background.

The headquarters building, originally called the administration building, was the nerve center of the fort throughout its existence. All matters pertaining to the daily business of running a military post were handled here. In this 1909 image, the cavalry riding hall can be seen on the far left.

Located on the east side of the main fort, the enlisted men's club served as an informal gathering place for soldiers. Unlike the stark, basic enlisted men's barracks seen below, this structure resembled a domestic residence, with smaller, intimate rooms and plenty of windows.

These enlisted men's barracks remained in use through World War II.

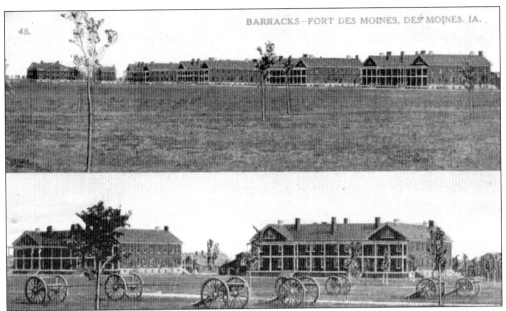

The upper panel of this split view of Fort Des Moines in 1905 features a view of the OCS barracks looking south across the parade ground. The lower panel shows cavalry cannons on the parade ground. The original caption on the back of this 1905 postcard reads, "Fort Des Moines is the latest and most up-to-date government post in the United States, being completed about 3 years ago. It is located 5 or 6 miles from the heart of the city."

These cavalry soldiers, seen on the parade ground in 1906, are preparing for deployment to Cuba in the aftermath of the Spanish-American War.

Cavalry regiments review on the parade ground around 1907.

This scene of cavalry regiments on the parade ground features the guardhouse, an original fort structure, on the right, and the headquarters building on the left. Additional OCS barracks line the far east side of the fort.

These cavalry stables, seen here in 1908, became barracks for the WAACs in 1942.

In 1917, 639 African American officers received their commissions at Fort Des Moines, a first in American military history.

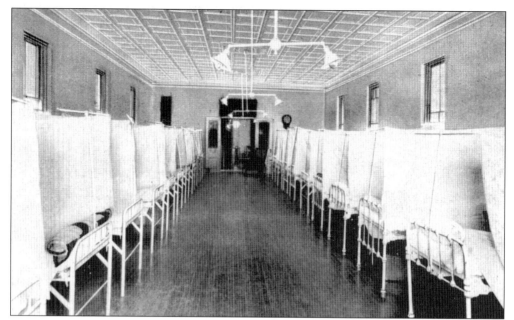

As wounded soldiers returned from European battlefields at the end of World War I, Fort Des Moines served as a hospital as well as training facility for medical personnel. This photograph is of one of many hospital wards at the fort.

Fort Des Moines Hospital 26, established in 1918, treated over 7,000 wounded soldiers before its closure in 1919. The hospital staff of officers featured here include, from left to right, (first row) Chaplain A. Richard Hedstrom, Capt. Joseph Hickson, Maj. George Watson, Col. George Juenemann, Capt. Peter Kuhn, Capt. Joe Carden, and Capt. Will Butler; (second row) Lt. Henry Price, Lt. William Henry, Lt. Yarnell Bowers, Lt. Ray Jones, and Lt. Fredrick Carpenter.

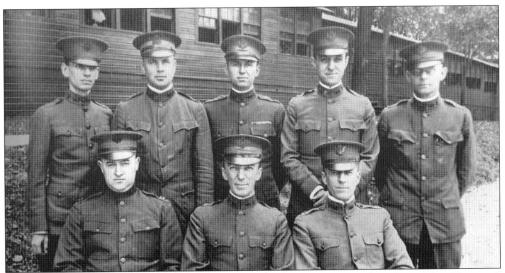

The medical and psychiatric staff at Hospital 26 in 1919 includes, from left to right, (first row) Capt. Patrick O'Farrell, Maj. Charles Barlow, and Capt. Lee Coffee; (second row) Lt. Herman Covey, Lt. Harry Lieffers, Capt. Charles Fallett, Lt. Elmer Eyman, and Lt. Ward Hedlund.

Practicing the most modern medical methods of psychiatric care available at the time, Fort Des Moines hospital staff encouraged psychiatric patients to seek outdoor physical activities such as gardening.

Regular exercise was also recommended for mentally traumatized patients. Medical records from 1919 indicate that 691 psychiatric cases were treated at Hospital 26, and the hospital took pride in its enlightened approach to their needs. For example, the use of physical restraints and chemical sedation was prohibited.

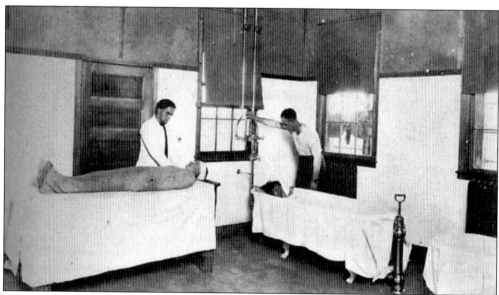

Relaxing hydrotherapy treatment, similar to modern whirlpool baths, provided calm and comfort to shell-shocked patients at the fort hospital.

Wounded soldiers regained dexterity making handicrafts at the fort hospital.

As a full-service hospital, Fort Des Moines offered a surgical and dental staff, as it would through World War II. In 1918, the staff includes, from left to right, (first row) Capt. Samuel Weitzman, Maj. Emmett Varvel, Maj. Harvard Moore, Lt. Col. Charles Havercampf, Maj. Joseph Greer, Maj. Stevens Brown, and Capt. Arthur Bratrud; (second row) Capt. Maximillion Bergeron, Capt. Lindsay Fletcher, Lt. John Armson, Lt. Karl Wahlberg, Capt. Robert Evans, Lt. Walter Jones, Lt. George Cox, and Lt. James Gorman.

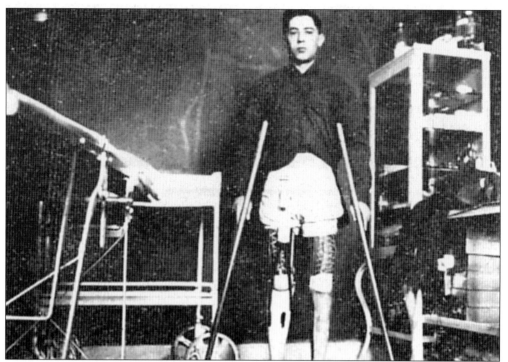

Fort Des Moines Hospital 26 treated over 3,500 patients in its orthopedic ward, 543 of whom were amputation cases.

From left to right, Sergeant Vonk and Sergeant Behrends with Corporal Cookley (first names unavailable) pose in front of the hospital ward in 1919.

The orthopedic doctors responsible for treating soldiers for serious limb wounds at Fort Des Moines in 1918 include, from left to right, (first row) Capt. Charles Ireland, Maj. Thomas Orr, Maj. Edward Parker, Maj. Eugene Stebbins, and Capt. Burgh Burnett; (second row) Capt. Charles Davis, Capt. Charles Llewellyn, Capt. John Wattenberg, Lt. Calvin DeBeck, and Lt. James Walker.

The physiotherapy staff at Fort Des Moines Hospital 26 administered treatments that included massage therapy, radiant heat application, and therapeutic exercise. Capt. Charles Ireland (front center) oversaw a staff of trained nurses. Pictured from left to right are (first row) Captain Ireland and Margaret Smith; (second row) Emma Hansen, Margaret Daubenspeck, and Stella-Marie Vincelli; (third row) Flora Scott, Signe Fossum, Edith Bonesteel, and Mrs. Walter Baker; (fourth row) Olive Scott, Jane Collier, and Clara Wolcott; (fifth row) Ruth Jessup, Ruth Reicheldorfer, and Alma Gephart.

The first unit of army nurses arrived at Fort Des Moines in the spring of 1918, but soon many were called away for overseas duty. In the fall of 1919, the number of nurses totaled 351, including those seen here (first names unavailable). Identified here are D. Fannin, N. Gibson, S. Stouffer, L. Keener, H. Peterson, L. Gleason, E. Cecil, M. Kelly, N. Hanson, D. Maxwell, A. Hanson, M. Greenless, A. Nugent, G. Pinkerton, K. Klebe, A. Gleason, H. Chestnut, G. Ryer, C. Canute, M. Aasen, F. Gibson, S. Crook, M. Zellman, M. Lennon, R. Kennedy, E. Miller, M. White, C. Berg, H. Kallen, A. Efta, C. Ollen, M. Johnson, M. Swanson, A. Redhead, M. Shiffer, B. Contwell, F. Sellgren, M. Corbitt, M. Owens, E. Boyd, E. Shaw, E. Curless, H. Farrel, A. Schultz, H. Steichen, A. Freund, L. Proske, G. Keener, C. Laubender, L. McNamara, S. Ball, and H. Taggert.

The Educational Services Administration was established in July 1918 at Fort Des Moines to provide classes in the psychological and statistical operations of a hospital, bedside occupations (techniques to rehabilitate disabled soldiers), technical skills (training with tools and machines), and agricultural programs (veterinary services, crops and soils, and animal husbandry). The Educational Services Administration in 1919 includes, from left to right, (first row) Lt. W. A. Cornell, Lt. W. E. Beanblossom, Capt. Harry Beck, Maj. Charles Berry, Capt. Victor Willitts, Lt. Charles Horn, and Lt. John Westrum; (second row) S. L. Scott, J. R. Haywood, D.E. Wiedman, Wm. Stone, E. J. Smith, and C. A. Bigbee; (third row) Sgt. Elmer Gehl, Sgt. Lester Peacock, Sgt. Arthur Rusted, Sgt. John Krachenbeuhl, Sgt. Joe Gramek, Pvt. Jacob, Brachle, and Sgt. Eiler Frederickson; (fourth row) Corp. George Zeller, Pvt. Victor Van Steenberg, Pvt. Dwight Harmount, Corp. George Klutho, and Sgt. Paul Christensen.

Reconstruction nurses' aides assisted patients in regaining physical strength and mobility and mental clarity through reading and studies. Seen here from 1919 are, from left to right, (first row) Mrs. C. L. Ireland, Ruth Robbins, Margaret Collins, Muriel Davis, Mary Wrinn, Grace Smith, Fannie Bacon, and Sarah Masterson; (second row) Floy Morgan, Jean Laird, Ethel Witty, Lillian Burnette, Gladys Burrows, Harriet Packard, and Frances Browne; (third row) Martha Granzow, Mrs. D. E. Wiedman, Erma Coons, Marjorie Morey, Louise Diehle, and Mary Porter; (fourth row) Ruth Wilcox, Charlotte Wilson, Ruth Pickell, Josephine Coldwell, Moel McFadden, Leah Henry, Edna Thompson, and Mollie Russell; (fifth row) Marion Brown, Mrs. Clyde Dampf, and Lois Maulsby.

Agriculture classes held at Fort Des Moines in 1919 were designed to give soldiers the tools to address the economic and practical challenges facing farmers in the postwar years.

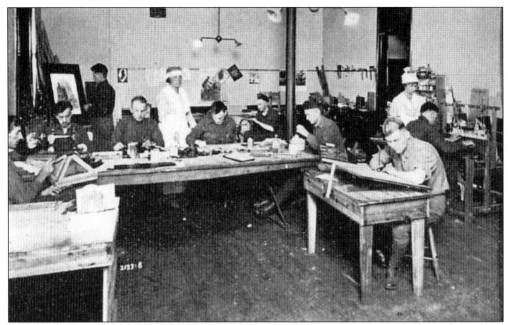

Craft shops were developed at the Fort Des Moines hospital to aide soldiers' recovery through diversion, recreation, and group interaction.

Convalescing patients practice their penmanship skills to prepare themselves for reentry into the business world.

The Automobile School at Fort Des Moines in 1919 offered classes in truck and tractor driving, storage battery repair, and starting, lighting, ignition, tire, and welding work.

Soldiers in 1919 enrolled in elementary business classes, including typing, in the fort's Educational Services Department.

The Quartermaster Corps in 1919 oversaw issues of transportation, supply, building upkeep, and road repair.

The Motor Transport Corps in 1919 consisted of 34 large trucks, 2 small trucks, 15 ambulances, and 4 passenger cars, all serving the hospital and fort patients and personnel.

The Personnel Office handled payroll issues at the fort hospital.

The army YMCA was the first welfare organization at Fort Des Moines. On Saturday nights, soldiers and hospital personnel could enjoy ice cream, cake, watermelon, doughnuts, and coffee. The YMCA also organized sporting events at the fort and held devotional services every Thursday and Sunday.

Realizing a growing need for reading material at Fort Des Moines, the main library was established in the summer of 1918. Most of its original holdings were donated by the public. The identities of the individuals featured in the circular insets are unknown.

The large general mess provided meals for the medical detachment in 1919, as well as the Quartermaster Corps and the Motor Transport Corps.

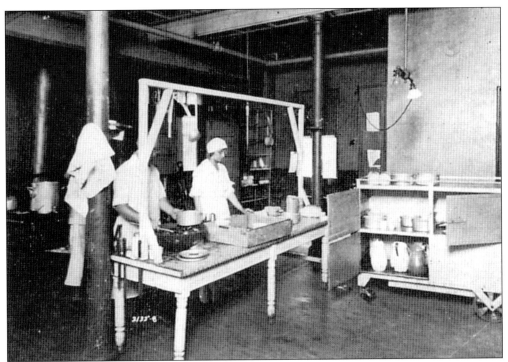

Eight additional kitchens and three special diet kitchens were opened at the fort by December 1918 to serve the growing patient population.

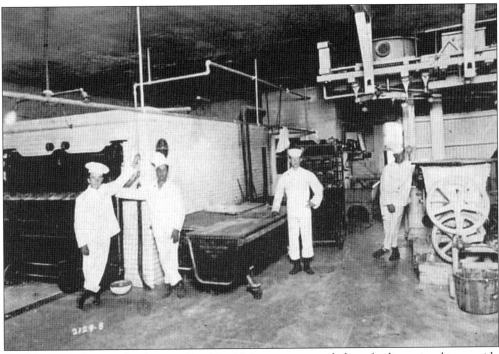

In addition to the nine kitchens at Fort Des Moines, a separate bakery facility existed to provide the seemingly endless loaves of bread and desserts for all mess tables.

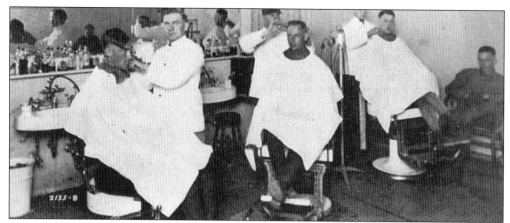

Fort Des Moines military personnel, staff, and patients had access to the post barbershop in 1919.

Medical personnel receive special decorations on the parade ground of Fort Des Moines in 1919 for their expertise in treating wounded soldiers.

In another award ceremony on the parade ground in 1919, medical personnel line up with the original post officers' quarters in the background.

The first baseball team from Hospital 26 was organized at Fort Des Moines in the spring of 1918. The team played other teams from Des Moines as well as other base hospital teams.

Personnel of Company A, Fort Des Moines Hospital 26, in 1919 pose in front of cavalry stable buildings.

Personnel of Company B, Fort Des Moines Hospital 26, in 1919 pose in front of enlisted men's barracks No. 2.

Personnel of Company C, Fort Des Moines Hospital 26, in 1919 pose in front of enlisted men's barracks.

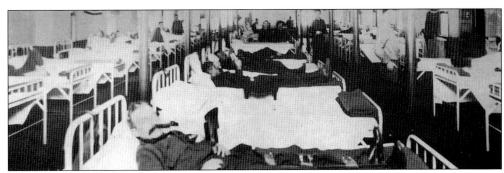

This hospital ward in 1919 remained in use, with much of the same equipment, through World War II.

Soldiers relax in their barracks in 1919.

This aerial view of Fort Des Moines in 1919 reveals the southeast corner of the post, featuring enlisted men's barracks on the left and the main hospital in the right foreground.

This view includes the south end of the Chaffee Road, the main post road leading off of the public Army Post Road, with a view of the YMCA building, the canteen, the main toolshed, and stable buildings. Beyond the toolshed in the area labeled "Camp Farm," Boomtown was built for the WAAC in 1942.

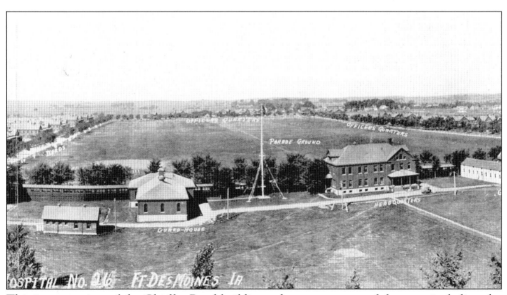

This is a rear view of the Chaffee Road buildings, the nerve center of the post, including the guardhouse, small stable, and headquarters. In the upper center, the parade ground is lined with officers' quarters.

The north end of the fort in 1919 features Clayton Hall near the main entrance, the Red Cross and gymnasium buildings, and noncommissioned officers' quarters on the far east. The huge riding hall, still in existence today, can be seen at the top right of the photograph.

Two

WORLD WAR II AND THE WOMEN'S ARMY CORPS
1942–1946

WAACs practiced drilling on the parade ground at Fort Des Moines in October 1942 with an enthusiasm and dedication that astounded their male counterparts. Long after sunset, WAACs could be found with flashlights on the parade ground, trying to perfect their formations. (National Archives.)

WAACs were brought from the Des Moines train station to Fort Des Moines by cattle trucks. They proceeded through the North Gate to begin their duty as the first female army auxiliaries in 1942. (Courtesy Women in Military Service for America.)

Once through the North Gate, WAACs saw the Chaffee Road buildings, including Clayton Hall, two theaters, the chapel, headquarters, the guardhouse, and the main post exchange, seen here in the right foreground.

Located on the southern side of the parade ground and seen here in March 1943, the barracks, used for male enlisted solders since cavalry days, were renovated to accommodate hundreds of WAAC officer candidates (Courtesy Women in Military Service for America.)

The renovation of these OCS barracks was minimal, including the installation of appropriate bathroom facilities. Still these accommodations proved woefully inadequate for the WAAC, with a ratio of 10 WAACs for every toilet available.

The OCS barracks featured a first-floor parlor area, sometimes including a piano, and a lower level where WAACs could enjoy a Coke or snack.

Planted in the cavalry days, the many mature trees lining the street in front of the OCS barracks provided some protection from the scorching heat of Des Moines summers.

Tree-lined Chaffee Road forms the eastern boundary of the expansive parade ground. (Courtesy Women in Military Service for America.)

This view of the parade ground, looking southeast, features a long line of OCS barracks.

Opposite the OCS barracks on the north and northwest side of the parade ground stand the many elegant officers' quarters from the cavalry days, still known as Officers' Row.

OFFICERS QUARTERS, FT. DES MOINES, IOWA

These two-story red brick officers' quarters featured columned verandas, spacious interior rooms, and large open hallways.

The lush tree-lined Officers' Row was one of the oldest sections of the fort.

OFFICERS QUARTERS. FT. DES MOINES. IOWA

This circle, known as Allen Circle, near the West Gate, formed the northwest area of Officers' Row, with a parklike knoll at the center.

In the far north corner of the fort, parallel to Army Post Road, a golf course provided a peaceful vista as well as recreation for those living on Officers' Row.

These stately officers' homes were divided into upper and lower apartments, each with a living room, a dining room, bedrooms, a bathroom, and a kitchen. Though the apartments were furnished, furniture and appliances were hard to come by during rationing, so many of the living and dining rooms remained sparsely furnished during the war years.

The West Gate of Fort Des Moines, near Officers' Row, was used less than the main North Gate but led directly to the gazebo-like bandstand on the parade ground.

The WAAC band performed on and near this bandstand on the parade ground, seen in 1942. (Courtesy Women in Military Service for America.)

This view of the bandstand features several OCS barracks on the south side of the parade ground.

The reviewing stand, used by military officers for observing and evaluating WAAC troops, was located adjacent to Officers' Row.

On the east side of the parade ground along Chaffee Road stood buildings that housed offices for the essential business of running the entire post, including the headquarters building (with the flagstaff in front), the guardhouse, and the main post exchange.

Scene,
Fort Des Moines.
Des Moines, Iowa.

This view of the Chaffee Road buildings takes the perspective from the North Gate. Clayton Hall, which served as the bachelors officers' quarters and officers' club, is the first building on the left. The parade ground is adjacent on the right.

20TH. CO., 3RD. REG., WAAC TRAINING CENTER, FORT DES MOINES, IOWA, NOVEMBER 12, 1
LT. W.W. KELLEY, BTLN. COMMANDER, LT. THERESA MRAVINTZ, 3RD. OFFICER, LT. JOHN SNOOK, TACTI
OFFICER

In September 1942, 20th Company, 3rd Regiment, of the WAAC, seated on bleachers in front of officers' quarters, was inducted. Each WAAC company and regiment was photographed in a similar manner. Note the "Hobby Hats," the first regulation WAAC cap, designed with a square top and visor and nicknamed after the director of the WAAC, Col. Oveta Culp Hobby. Other components of the first WAAC army-issued attire can be seen here as well: the overcoats, many of which were in sizes much too large for most of the women, and the durable, comfortable, but universally unflattering shoes, which the WAACs quickly nicknamed "the gruesome two-somes" for their ability to make any woman's legs look like stovepipes.

On July 18, 1944, 5th Company, 1st Regiment, sits for its group photograph in front of OCS barracks. (Courtesy Women in Military Service for America.)

WAACs pose by the cannon in front of the guardhouse in March 1943. (Courtesy Women in Military Service for America.)

One of the original buildings at the fort, the guardhouse sported a narrow porch with low railings and a sign hanging over its front stairs identifying the building. The guardhouse served as the office for the military police and a jailhouse.

Offices located in the headquarters building were arguably the busiest at the fort. Headquarters contained the offices of the commandant of the post, the adjutant general, the Signal Corps, the WAAC training commander, post administration, and field director of the Red Cross, as well as the post's radio and telegraph station.

As if to designate the importance of the headquarters building, the flagstaff adorned its south lawn. As was traditional on all army posts, the flagstaff and headquarters faced the parade ground.

The chapel (left) and old post theater (right) were located north of headquarters on Chaffee Road. First-run films ran in the theater, as well as training films. The chapel, built in 1910 and still standing today, held services in nearly every denomination. Red brick with white trim and topped with a Celtic cross, the chapel exterior also features stained-glass windows on each side, traditional windows on the front on either side of the white, Gothic front door, and a pointed roof mimicking the shape of the doorway.

One of the oldest buildings at the fort, the main post exchange (PX No. 1) was by far the most popular destination on payday. A kind of military department store, the post exchange provided for all of a WAAC's needs, from cosmetics to candy, all at bargain prices specially set for military personnel.

The two-story main post exchange featured a grill/sandwich counter, a tailor and shoe-shine shop, and a serve-yourself store where WAACs could select their soaps, toothpaste, cosmetics, magazines, candy, and postcards. Each morning, fresh homemade chocolate doughnuts and fresh coffee was the most frequently ordered breakfast. Behind the post exchange, a hairdresser's shop created regulation (off-the-collar) hairstyles for the WAACs. (Courtesy Woltz Photo.)

Christmas in wartime is always melancholy, but a visit to the main post exchange could brighten the season. For Christmas 1943, festive streamers and a large icicle-strewn Christmas tree adorn the interior of the post exchange. Even Santa's house beckons homesick WAACs and GIs with the message "Keep your date with Santa." (Courtesy Woltz Photo.)

Hospital ~ Fort Des Moines, Iowa

Fort Des Moines's long history as a military hospital, seen here in 1941, continued into the WAAC period. Soldiers, mostly from the African campaign, were flown into the Des Moines airport for treatment at the fort hospital before being transferred to Fitzsimmons General Hospital in Denver, Colorado.

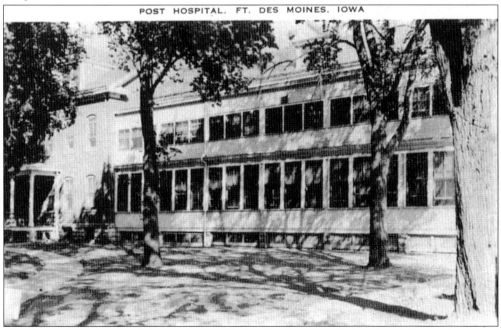

POST HOSPITAL. FT. DES MOINES. IOWA

The hospital at Fort Des Moines during World War II was staffed with a full complement of doctors, ear, nose, and throat specialists, dentists, nurses, and civil service assistants. New buildings were erected near the original hospital to accommodate the growing number of casualties treated at the fort.

The combination post office/fire department (Building 87), located at the southern end of the original post area of Chaffee Road, was constructed in 1905 and still stands today. It once served as a cavalry bandstand and polo stable, which held up to 60 cavalry horses. (Courtesy Women in Military Service for America.).

Quarters 400, one of several prefabricated buildings added to the original post area during the WAAC period, housed WAAC officers who worked in the essential Chaffee Road buildings, including the post exchange, headquarters, motor pool, and so on. Quarters 400 was located behind headquarters.

The consolidated mess stood amid Stable Row. It was the largest of the mess halls, accommodating 2,000 personnel for meals.

By 1943, Fort Des Moines boasted a total of 14 fully equipped, fully functional mess halls. (Courtesy Women in Military Service for America.)

The officers' mess served the smallest number of diners, approximately 150. (Courtesy Women in Military Service for America.)

The two service clubs at Fort Des Moines were located near the entrance to Boomtown. Staffed by civilian hostesses, the service clubs provided as atmosphere of relaxation and recreation for WAACs.

Many activities were offered to WAACs at the service clubs. They could entertain guests (even male guests, who were not allowed in the barracks), eat at the cafeteria, play piano in the music appreciation room, dance in the dance hall, play bingo or Monopoly, or sing in the glee club. (Courtesy Women in Military Service for America.)

In service club No. 1, a huge wall mural graced the area above an interior doorway. Painted by 2nd Officer Lorraine R. Marshall and Technician 5th Grade Eleanor Robertson, the mural depicted the many behind-the-scenes jobs that the WAAC and WAC accomplished in order to "free a man to fight." Note the WAC at the top center of the mural passing a rifle to a soldier in the battlefield. The other scenes in the mural represent the various jobs the WAC filled: cooking, administration, motor transport, film work and photography, and map reading. (Courtesy Women in Military Service for America.)

Clayton Hall was one of the first buildings a WAAC saw upon arrival through the North Gate at Fort Des Moines. During World War II, Clayton Hall served as the bachelor officers' quarters as well as an officers' club. Nestled amid mature trees and shrubbery, it was one of the most beautiful buildings at the fort. Unmarried officers lived on the first and second floors. Downstairs (the basement level) an officers' club offered music and drinks for male and WAAC officers. Visiting dignitaries, such as First Lady Eleanor Roosevelt in 1943, were received at Clayton Hall.

Stable St. W.A.E. Training Center. Ft. Des Moines Ia.

When the WAAC first arrived at Fort Des Moines, the existing barracks proved insufficient for their numbers. To accommodate all of the new WAAC recruits, the cavalry stables were hurriedly converted into barracks, including the addition of porches, seen here. Still the legacy of the cavalry days lived on; in many cases, the musty smell of horseflesh lingered in the air, and wagon wheels still hung from the ceiling beams. In a satiric homage to their director, Col. Oveta Culp Hobby, and their new surroundings, the WAACs who lived in the converted stables took to calling themselves "Hobby Horses."

Despite renovations, these long, narrow, peaked-roof stables remained quite stark compared to the OCS barracks. The small windows offered little sense of space or exterior views.

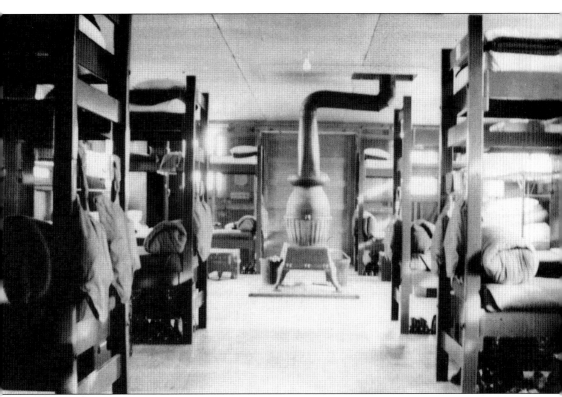

Although new heaters were installed, the stable barracks could be cold and drafty during the bitter Des Moines winters. (Courtesy Women in Military Service for America.)

Cots were assembled in the stables, and new floors, partly new walls, and modern lighting and plumbing facilities made the stables suitable barracks for the WAACs, seen here on August 14, 1942. (Courtesy Des Moines Register and Tribune.)

This view of Thayer Street represents the length of Stable Row, flanked on the right by OCS barracks. (Courtesy U.S. Army Women's Museum, Fort Lee, Virginia.)

Originally named the Winn Area after a famous artillery officer, Gen. John S. Winn, Boomtown referred to the buildings on the south end of the post constructed in response to the need for additional space and facilities for the WAAC. Boomtown's 174 mostly tile buildings were designated T (temporary) structures, designed to go up quickly and come down as soon as they had served their purpose. Within a period of five months in 1942, Fort Des Moines experienced more growth than it had known in the previous 50 years, at a cost of approximately $2 million. This September 7, 1942, view of Boomtown shows the white classroom buildings on the upper left, the service clubs on the lower left, the clothing warehouse and motor garage on the right front, and rows of barracks along the upper right. (Courtesy Des Moines Register and Tribune.)

The Boomtown mess hall, seen here on September 3, 1942, accommodated 150 WAACs. The foundation of this building, like many Boomtown structures, was laid in one day, with the entire building completed in two weeks. (Courtesy Des Moines Register and Tribune.)

When completed, Boomtown ultimately provided more than 50 barracks, an administration building, several mess halls, a library, a chapel, huge motion picture halls with the latest projection equipment, classroom buildings, and the new post exchange (PX No. 2), seen here under construction on August 14, 1942. (Courtesy Des Moines Register and Tribune.)

The new post exchange in Boomtown, like its larger, older counterpart, featured a long soda fountain, seen here, as well as a tailor shop, doughnut machine, toiletries, magazines, cigarettes, and cosmetics. (Courtesy Woltz Photo.)

The new post exchange (right) was located next to the Boomtown chapel (left). This chapel was much simpler in design than the original post chapel. With its exterior of white wood and traditional steeple, this chapel resembled an old country church.

Boomtown barracks went up amid the mud and snow of the transitional fall-to-winter weather of Des Moines in 1942. These barracks housed the WAAC 3rd Platoon, 4th Company, 3rd Regiment, in March 1943. (Courtesy Women in Military Service for America.)

Eventually, the mud of Boomtown disappeared, covered with seed and soil or paved walkways. WAAC 4th Company resided in these barracks in March 1943. (Courtesy Women in Military Service for America.)

The 9th Company, 3rd Regiment, 73rd Basic Company, appears here marching on the Boomtown parade ground on March 21, 1944. Those in charge of the company include Lieutenant Keogh and Lieutenant Iskowitz, platoon commanders; Lieutenant Smith, company commander; Lieutenant Foster, second in command; and Lieutenant Collins, platoon commander. (Courtesy Women in Military Service for America.)

By the end of 1943, every building on the old cavalry post, as well as the new Boomtown area, was occupied by women who had enlisted in the army to do their part in the largest military conflict in human history. At its peak, Fort Des Moines supported approximately 14,000 WAC personnel. (Courtesy Women in Military Service for America.)

Three

MARCHING INTO HISTORY
THE LIFE OF A FORT DES MOINES
WAAC/WAC

This "Spirit of the WAAC" postcard includes a description of this image as "a miniature representation of a giant photo mural . . . dedicated to the WAAC . . . on permanent display in the main banking room of the Central National Bank & Trust Company, Des Moines, Iowa."

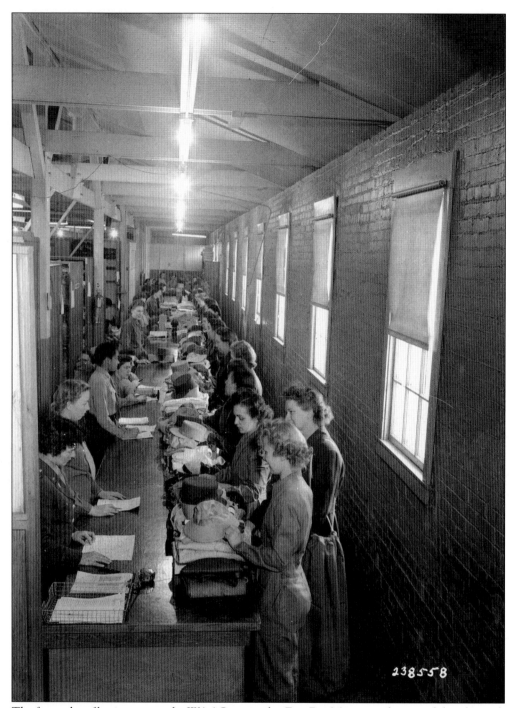

The first order of business once the WAACs arrived at Fort Des Moines and received their barrack assignments was to obtain their uniforms. Here WAC recruits line up at the Quartermaster to receive their regulation clothing on February 17, 1944. (National Archives.)

This WAC recruit is fitted for her army-issue hat. (Courtesy Women in Military Service for America.)

Exchanges in clothing were often necessary to obtain properly fitted uniforms, and WAACs stand in line at the quartermaster's hoping to receive clothing more true to size. (Courtesy Women in Military Service for America.)

Since the army was caught by surprise by the number of WAAC recruits, as well as the early winter of 1942, men's overcoats were issued to the women in October 1942. (Courtesy Women in Military Service for America.)

Not discouraged by her overwhelming attire, WAAC Alice Manning bravely salutes in her enlisted man's coat in 1942. (Courtesy Women in Military Service for America.)

Eventually the men's overcoats were replaced with properly fitted WAAC coats and uniforms. Here WACs pose in front of the cannon across from headquarters in 1943. (Courtesy Women in Military Service for America.)

The WAAC summer uniform consisted of khaki-colored jackets, skirts, shirts, and ties, as well as a matching "Hobby Hat" and the "gruesome two-some" shoes. These OCS candidates pose near their barracks in August 1942. (Courtesy Women in Military Service for America.)

WAACs in 1942 delighted in their new winter uniforms in "OD" (olive drab) with "Hobby Hats."

OCS candidates pose in their summer uniforms in front of the cannon in 1942. (Courtesy Women in Military Service for America.)

Winter in Des Moines can be severe, and WACs were provided with appropriate outerwear to fend off the cold in 1944. (Courtesy Women in Military Service for America.)

WAACs engage in daily calisthenics on the parade ground in 1942. (Courtesy Women in Military Service for America.)

The WAAC band practices marching through Officers' Row. (Courtesy Women in Military Service for America.)

THE WAAC'S OWN BAND PARADES AT A TRAINING CENTER

The WAACs were extremely proud of their own band, and they often lined the parade ground to watch the band in action.

Although WACs were not assigned to combat duty, they were required to learn basic defense actions, such as pistol firing. Here WACs train in small arms target practice at Fort Des Moines around 1944.

The WAAC bugler signaled the beginning of each day and closed each evening with the plaintive sound of taps.

WACs line up at the consolidated mess hall on Stable Row around 1943.

The WAAC cooks and bakers at Fort Des Moines receive a surprise visitor, Hollywood actor Robert Young. (Courtesy Women in Military Service for America.)

WAAC cooks and bakers stand outside one of the smaller mess halls, mess No. 2. (Courtesy Women in Military Service for America.)

Lt. Carrie A. LeFew performs her desk duties as part of her job at PX No. 2 in Boomtown around 1943. Lieutenant LeFew, like many WACs, served to help shorten the war and bring loved ones home from battle. Note the photograph of Lieutenant LeFew's husband on the desk. Tragically, her husband was killed on Corregidor in the Philippines.

WAACs took great pride in their ability to drill with precision.

WAACs stand in formation on the parade ground in 1942.

Commanding officers at Fort Des Moines included Col. Don Faith (right), seen here with WAAC director Col. Oveta Culp Hobby (center) and Colonel Morgan.

A WAC company in "eyes right" formation marches with the WAC band on the parade ground around 1943.

WAACs perform drill formation in review on the parade ground around 1943.

The leader of the winning WAC company in review receives accolades around 1943.

WACs march in review on the parade ground. The WAC band can be seen in the inset photograph, taken around 1943.

WACs stand at ease in front of Officers' Row in 1944. (Courtesy Women in Military Service for America.)

In 1944, WACs stand at attention for review. (Courtesy Women in Military Service for America.)

WACs salute in formation in 1944. (Courtesy Women in Military Service for America.)

WACs face the parade ground at attention in 1944. (Courtesy Women in Military Service for America.)

WAACs gather for formation outside of the OCS barracks lining the south side of the parade ground in 1942. (Courtesy Women in Military Service for America.)

Male officers trained WAACs at Fort Des Moines until a sufficient number of female officers was commissioned, around 1942.

Male officers and enlisted men join WAACs in formation on the parade ground around 1942.

One of the many male officers assigned to train the WAACs, Major Fowler leaves a WAAC company after a surprise barracks inspection. Note the long overcoats the women are wearing to conceal their incomplete uniforms. (Courtesy Women in Military Service for America.)

OCS candidates graduate in July 1943.

WACs attend an outdoor class on the parade ground in 1943. The bleachers were moved to a location under the trees to offset the effects of the oppressive heat of a Des Moines summer. Even WAC summer uniforms were nearly unbearable in the humidity and direct sunshine. (Courtesy Women in Military Service for America.)

On September 30, 1943, the WAAC was abolished, and all members who wished to stay in the military became members of the WAC, no longer auxiliaries but members of the "regular army" of the United States, with the same titles, ranks, pay scale, and so on. More than 41,000 enlisted women chose to stay in the WAC, and almost 5,000 officers accepted commissions in the new organization. Here former WAACs are sworn in as WACs. (National Archives.)

The 10th Company graduates in 1944.

A WAC company on the parade ground salutes the colors.

The WAC band performs at a WAC graduation day parade in 1944.

COMPANY 24, 3RD REG., MVO 8'S, 1st WAC TRAINING CENTER, FORT DES MOINES, IOWA - 28 OCTOBER 1944

While the military as a whole was largely segregated, African American and white WACs often served together in the same company. Here Company 24, 3rd Regiment, Motor Vehicle Operators pose in front of the OCS barracks on October 28, 1944. (Courtesy Women in Military Service for America.)

WACs pose in fatigue uniforms in 1943. (Courtesy Rosemary Reed Powell.)

WACs relax in fatigues outside of Boomtown barracks. (Courtesy Rosemary Reed Powell.)

Time weighed heavily on WACs in the evenings and holidays when they had time to worry about loved ones. Christmas was particularly lonesome and stressful, as the faces of these Fort Des Moines WACs reveal. These WACs lived in Quarters 400, one of the few Boomtown-style temporary buildings erected in the old fort area. One of the advantages of living in Quarters 400 was the luxury of privacy (each officer had her own room) and the opportunity to decorate one's room according to personal taste.

Unexpected wintertime recreation for a WAC (Lieutenant Smith-Robinson) could come in the form of "skating" down the roads connecting the riding hall (upper right) to the hospital area. (Courtesy Rosemary Reed Powell.)

WACs are sworn in on the parade ground near the bandstand area in 1943. The hospital is seen in the background.

WACs take the oath of service in 1943.

Artist Max Halverson began drawing cartoons of military life when he was a young man of 17 living in Des Moines. Although he would later serve in the military himself and draw many cartoons of life in the service, among his first subjects were the WAACs of Fort Des Moines. (Courtesy Max Halverson.)

Four

FINAL CALL TO DUTY
FORT DES MOINES SINCE 1946

When World War II ended, Fort Des Moines remained a bustling center of demobilization and separation, but on December 15, 1945, its role as a WAC training center came to an end. On April 16, 1946, the last WAC left Fort Des Moines. Faced with the prospect of devoting huge amounts of funds to the upkeep of the original post buildings, the government chose to destroy most of the buildings at Fort Des Moines. Here the original post exchange is demolished on July 13, 1960. The men of Company A-495, Engineer Battalion, from Keokuk, Iowa, completed the demolition while on two week's army reserve training. (Courtesy Des Moines Register and Tribune.)

In February 1957, the entire area of Boomtown was destroyed, as seen here in this February 21, 1957, photograph. A zoo occupies part of the area today, as well as some reserve training facilities. (Courtesy Des Moines Register and Tribune.)

The WAC commissary on Rodgers Road once served as a granary in the fort's cavalry days. This building, seen here in 1986, no longer exists. (Photograph by Larry Day; courtesy Library of Congress.)

The Quartermaster building, seen here in 1986, was torn down in the late 1980s. (Photograph by Larry Day; courtesy Library of Congress.)

The WAAC motor transport building No. 126 originally housed cavalry mules. By the 1980s, it fell into ruin and was destroyed. (Photograph by Larry Day; courtesy Library of Congress.)

These OCS barracks, No. 55 and No. 56, still stand today but are boarded up and quickly deteriorating. (Photograph by Larry Day; courtesy Library of Congress.)

This interior view of OCS barracks No. 56 in 1986 shows the beginnings of the building's deterioration. (Photograph by Larry Day; courtesy Library of Congress.)

While some of the WAC OCS barracks have been renovated into modern condominiums, those shown here in 1986 are no longer safe to enter and have been boarded up. (Photograph by Larry Day; courtesy Library of Congress.)

This exterior view of OCS barracks No. 58 in 1986 shows the lower level partially boarded up.

This is the last photograph, taken in 2001, of the entrance door to an OCS barracks. Shortly after this photograph and the following were taken, no further access to these buildings was permitted.

This is the last photograph, taken in 2001, of the interior of an original OCS barracks, dating back to cavalry days.

This former cavalry stable (No. 86) and WAAC clothing warehouse still stands, though boarded up.

Stable No. 71, shown here in 1986, is now boarded up. (Photograph by Larry Day; courtesy Library of Congress.)

This interior view of stable No. 71 from 1986 reveals the deterioration of this old cavalry structure, once used as a WAAC barracks. (Photograph by Larry Day; courtesy Library of Congress.)

This cavalry office and supply building still stands but is boarded up. (Photograph by Larry Day; courtesy Library of Congress.)

This single-horse stable, originally located behind headquarters, was the only stable on Chaffee Road. The smallest building among the old post structures, this stable still stands today in fairly good condition.

Officers' Row has suffered the same fate as the OCS barracks. Listed on the National Registry of Historic Places, these buildings cannot be destroyed unless they become a public hazard. Officers' quarters No. 14 and No. 15 have continued to deteriorate since this photograph was taken in 1986. (Photograph by Larry Day; courtesy Library of Congress.)

This boarded up officers' quarters, seen here in 1986, still stands on the once majestic Officers' Row. (Photograph by Larry Day; courtesy Library of Congress.)

This interior view of an officer's quarters from 1986 hints of the stately elegance of an earlier time. When quarters like these were destroyed after World War II, holes were drilled in the first-floor ceilings to allow all of the furniture in the second floor apartments to come crashing down, expediting the demolition process. (Photograph by Larry Day; courtesy Library of Congress.)

Seen here in 1986, the recreation/riding hall remains in constant use today as part of the naval reserve center at the fort. (Photograph by Larry Day; courtesy Library of Congress.)

Building No. 87 once served as the post office and fire department at the post during World War II. Today it is used by a private company.

Clayton Hall, pictured here in 1986, was once the bachelors officers' quarters and officers' club. After World War II, it became a naval recruiting center. Today it is one of the two major buildings that form the Fort Des Moines Memorial Park and Education Center. Clayton Hall has been completely upgraded and remodeled, keeping the original style on the exterior and creating a modern museum inside. The three-story museum honors all who served at the fort, from the buffalo soldiers and cavalry to the WAC. (Photograph by Larry Day; courtesy Library of Congress.)

The chapel is the other major building to serve as a central part of the Fort Des Moines Memorial Park and Education Center. By the early 1980s, the chapel seemed doomed to the same fate as so many other Fort Des Moines buildings when Col. Louis Erbstein, curator of the Fort Des Moines Museum, launched a campaign to save it from destruction. Colonel Erbstein asked former WAACs and WACs to write letters to the appropriate government and military officials, asking them to fund the restoration of the chapel where the women had spent so many years praying for the safe return of loved ones and an end to war. The campaign proved successful, and the chapel, seen here in 1986, is now a beautiful jewel in the fort's memorial park. (Photograph by Larry Day; courtesy Library of Congress.)

The chapel once faced the expansive parade ground. Since the mid-1980s, modern apartment buildings line what once was the east side of the parade ground. (Photograph by Larry Day; courtesy Library of Congress.)

The interior of the restored chapel pictured here in 1986 replicates exactly the chapel in which the WACs worshipped. The same number of pews lines the sides of the center aisle, the same angels adorn the arched ceiling, the same Gothic stained-glass windows line the side of the walls, and the same Rosetta glass crowns the altar. (Photograph by Larry Day; courtesy Library of Congress.)

This 1986 close-up of the Rosetta altar window reveals some of the beauty and detail in the glasswork. (Photograph by Larry Day; courtesy Library of Congress.)

The West Gate, seen here in 1986, is being rebuilt as part of the fort's current renovation. Original stones from the gate will be used to reconstruct the new entrance. (Photograph by Larry Day; courtesy Library of Congress.)

"We learned and grew and were transformed not so much by what we did, but by why and how we did it."

In the memorial park between the chapel and Clayton Hall, a memorial wall stands. The inscription reads, "We learned and grew and were transformed, not so much by what we did but by why and how we did it." In front of the wall, inlaid stones feature the names of many who served at the fort.

This artist's rendering of the Fort Des Moines Memorial Park and Education Center features Clayton Hall at the north and the chapel at the south. The memorial park includes two reflecting pools connected by an abstract bronze sculpture by artist Richard Hunt. The base of the statue will include the names of the 639 graduate captains and lieutenants from 1917 and the first 436 WAAC officers from 1942. The Fort Des Moines Memorial Park and Education Center opened to the public in 2004. (Courtesy Fort Des Moines Memorial Park and Education Center.)

BIBLIOGRAPHY

Bellafaire, Judith A. *The Women's Army Corps: A Commemoration of World War II Service.* Washington, DC: U.S. Army Center of Military History, Government Printing Office, 1993. http://www.army.mil/cmh-pg/brochures/wac/wac.htm.

Bessey, Carol Hossner. *Battle of the WAC.* Kearney, NE: Morris, 1999.

Blake, Penelope A. *My Mother's Fort.* North Charleston, NC: BookSurge Publishing, 2005.

Clark, Blake. "Ladies of the Army." *Readers' Digest* 42, no. 253 (May 1943): 85–88. Previously published in *New York Times* (April 11, 1943).

Gill, Dottie. *A Secret Place in My Heart: A Diary of a World War II WAC.* San Jose, CA: Writers Club, 2000.

Grahn, Elna Hilliard. *In the Company of Waacs.* Manhattan, KS: Sunflower University Press, 1993.

Lewis, Brenda Ralph. *Women at War.* Pleasantville, NY: Readers' Digest/Amber Books, 2002.

Litoff, Judy Barrett, and David C. Smith. *We're in This War, Too: World War II Letters from American Women in Uniform.* New York: Oxford University Press, 1994.

Miller, Grace Porter. *Call of Duty: A Montana Girl in World War II.* Baton Rouge, LA: Louisiana State University Press, 1999.

Morden, Col. Betty J. "Women's Army Corps: WAAC and WAC." In *In Defense of a Nation: Servicewomen in World War II,* edited by Major General Jeanne M. Holm, 39–55. Arlington, VA: Vandamere, 1998.

Nicely, Marian. *The Ladies' First Army.* Ligonier, PA: Fairfield Street, 1989.

Offenburger, Chuck. *Babe: An Iowa Legend.* Ames, IA: Iowa State University Press, 1989.

Pollard, Clarice F. *Laugh, Cry and Remember: The Journal of a G.I. Lady.* Phoenix: Journeys, 1991.

Pollock, Elizabeth and Ruth Duhme. *Yes Ma'am!: The Personal Papers of a WAAC Private.* Philadelphia: Lippincott, 1943.

Robinson, Harriet Green. *The Gaylord WACS.* Laguna Beach, CA: Laurel, 2001.

Rosenthal, Rose. *Not All Soldiers Wore Pants.* Rochelle Park, NJ: Ryzell, 1993.

Shea, Nancy. *The Waacs.* New York: Harper, 1943.

Treadwell, Mattie E. *The Women's Army Corps.* Washington, DC: U.S. Army Center of Military History, Government Printing Office, 1954.

Weatherford, Doris. *American Women and World War II.* New York: Facts on File, 1990.

Williams, Vera. *WACS: Women's Army Corps.* Osceola, WI: Motorbooks, 1997.

Women's Army Corps Veterans Association. *Daughters of Pallas Athene: Cameo Recollections of Women's Army Corps Veterans.* Independence, MO: Print America, 1983.

INDEX

ACROSS AMERICA, PEOPLE ARE DISCOVERING SOMETHING WONDERFUL. THEIR HERITAGE.

Arcadia Publishing is the leading local history publisher in the United States. With more than 3,000 titles in print and hundreds of new titles released every year, Arcadia has extensive specialized experience chronicling the history of communities and celebrating America's hidden stories, bringing to life the people, places, and events from the past. To discover the history of other communities across the nation, please visit:

www.arcadiapublishing.com

Customized search tools allow you to find regional history books about the town where you grew up, the cities where your friends and family live, the town where your parents met, or even that retirement spot you've been dreaming about.

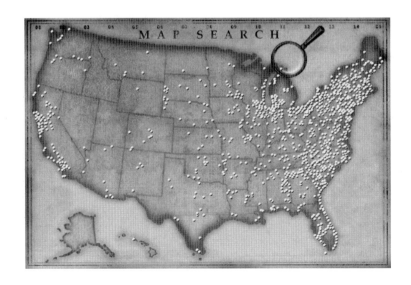